100 Days
of Thanking
HASHEM

*Build Your Spiritual Capacity For
Gratitude One Day At A Time*

RIVKAH LAMBERT ADLER

100 Days of Thanking Hashem
Published by Geula Watch Press, Jerusalem, ISRAEL

© 2020 Rivkah Lambert Adler

ISBN: 978-0-9993789-2-2

INTRODUCTION

There are dozens of gratitude journals available. What makes this one different?

When *Leah Imenu* (our mother Leah) the first wife of *Yaakov Avinu* (our father Jacob) gave birth to her fourth son, she named him *Yehuda*. The name *Yehuda* is derived from the Hebrew verb *l'hodot*, which means to thank.

The Jewish people are referred to in Hebrew as *Yehudim*. **In a fundamental way, to be a Jew means to be grateful.** The trait is embedded in our very name.

Indeed, an important spiritual task is to notice and appreciate the kindnesses that *Hashem* (God) performs for us all day long. This journal will help you build your spiritual muscle of gratitude one day at a time. At the end of your 100 days with this journal, thanking Hashem will be a well-honed muscle and a way for you to connect with Hashem easily and often.

There's a tradition in Judaism to recite 100 *brachot* (blessings that begin with the words *Baruch Atah*) a day. Those who pray three times a day can get most of these *brachot* in during formal prayer. Add to that the blessings said before and after eating and after using the bathroom and for most people in this category, hitting 100 *brachot* a day is pretty doable.

Even if you don't happen to be a Jew who prays three times a day, there is another way to express your thanks to God for all the blessings you have. This journal will help you get there.

This all started for me some years ago when, at night, just before nodding off, I would thank Hashem for ten things that I appreciated from that day. Thank you Hashem that

I found a parking space downtown. Thank you Hashem that my sister called today. Thank you Hashem that I had time to finish reading the novel I was so enjoying, etc.

Mindful of this teaching about 100 *brachot* a day, I decided to take it up a notch and thank Hashem for 100 specific things I appreciate.

I keep track by taking a book, putting my hand on page 1 and saying, "Thank you Hashem for ..." Then I put my hand on page 2 and thank Hashem for something else. And so on, until I reach page 100.

I created this Jewish gratitude journal to encourage you to take on the spiritual practice of gratitude. I included two features that I hope will help you get into the habit of thanking Hashem.

First, I know that expressing 100 gratitudes at a time can seem overwhelming. With this journal, you will start slowly. On Day 1, you only have to thank Hashem for one thing. By Day 10, you will be better able to find 10 things for which to express gratitude to Hashem.

Imagine what you'll be able to do by Day 100 and every day after, having built your spiritual muscle, one day at a time!

I've included lots of inspiring quotes from Jewish sources, from the Bible and from non-Jewish thinkers who expressed something worth considering about gratitude. Finally, the journal is full of gratitude prompts – things to consider that will help you complete your daily list of gratitudes.

To further inspire you, here's a list of 100 things for which I wanted to thank Hashem. If any of these apply to you, you're welcome to include them in your list, but mostly it's to inspire you to realize how many *brachot* Hashem literally showers us with every moment.

Thank you Hashem for:
1. the ability to see color
2. clean dishes
3. my fully-stocked spice drawer

4. the ability to read
5. books
6. my children
7. my English vocabulary
8. my 10 fingers that all work
9. not being in a hospital bed
10. medicine when I have pain
11. not needing to save the carrot and potato peels to eat
12. the wireless speaker that plays my favorite music when I cook for Shabbat
13. Shabbat
14. guests for Shabbat
15. letting me live in Israel
16. the abundance of kosher food wherever I go in Israel
17. a home of my own
18. my amazing husband
19. being able to breath without assistance
20. tickets to a concert I've been wanting to see
21. the fact that no one I love died yesterday
22. hot pizza
23. cold water
24. an app that tells me when my bus is coming
25. mild weather
26. the ability to make money
27. students to teach
28. teachers from whom I can learn
29. the ability to cry
30. hugs
31. shoes for every kind of activity I want to do
32. friends who understand what I'm feeling
33. technology that lets me see the faces of people who live far away when I talk to them
34. my new green dress
35. memories
36. birthdays
37. sweet white wine
38. breeze

39. the ability to walk all around a deserted parking lot after midnight looking for our car and finding it and having it start and getting home safely
40. the way we sing at our table on Shabbat
41. *bentsching* my children on Friday night
42. my grandson's growing vocabulary
43. novels that make me cry when they end
44. the ability to read Hebrew
45. personal growth
46. the prayers and chapters of *Tehillim* I know by heart
47. our car
48. the long-awaited check that finally arrived
49. self-confidence
50. knowing *Birkat haMazon* by heart
51. friends who confide in me
52. the fact that I don't have any desire to smoke
53. the ability to talk to You whenever I want
54. air travel
55. rain
56. the moments when I can actually feel my soul growing
57. my black Uggs
58. a climate-controlled home
59. the view from my back porch
60. photographs and digital images
61. the ability to hire people to do the jobs I can't or don't want to do
62. my kitchen
63. clients who pay on time
64. yellow peppers
65. the ability to teach adults
66. deep, meaningful conversations
67. faces I love
68. the technical skills I have
69. tissues
70. the way my heart aches when I miss someone
71. pasta
72. Jerusalem
73. my *teudat zehut* (Israeli citizenship papers)

74. my Israeli passport
75. my Israeli driver's license
76. pancakes
77. friends who are working on themselves
78. the ability to write what some people want to read
79. cheesy kale chips
80. days when all my technology works
81. simple solutions that make problems go away
82. the combination of olive green, burgundy and beige
83. breathing hard and sweating but not having a heart attack
84. floating on my back in the pool
85. our dishwasher
86. the fact that the *Kotel* and *Kever Rachel* are just a short drive away
87. my modest bathing suit
88. our icemaker
89. that I don't have a life-threatening illness
90. glasses that correct my vision
91. nails to scratch my skin when it itches
92. the ability to speak in funny accents
93. my loud laugh
94. the ability to love
95. forks
96. having just the right book to lend out
97. a flexible schedule
98. vacation
99. fans in the summer
100. movies

Now it's your turn. Turn the page and let's get started!

DAY 1

Thank You Hashem for:

1.

"Gratitude turns what we have into enough." — Anonymous

DAY 2

Thank You Hashem for:

1.

2.

> "Feeling grateful to Hashem is indeed our most important task. We build a steadfast connection by way of our gratitude to Him. Therefore, as long as our gratitude to Hashem is deficient, our connection to Hashem remains weak and incomplete." - Rabbi Shalom Arush, Garden of Gratitude, p. 135

DAY
3

Thank You Hashem for:

1.

2.

3.

Gratitude prompt: *What was broken that is now fixed and functional?*

DAY 4

Thank You Hashem for:

1.

2.

3.

4.

I will thank You forever and ever when You have done
[this], and I will hope for Your name, for it is good, in the
presence of Your devoted ones. (Tehillim 52:11)

DAY
5

Thank You Hashem for:

1.

2.

3.

4.

5.

Gratitude prompt: *What technology have you mastered well enough to benefit from?*

DAY 6

Thank You Hashem for:

1.

2.

3.

4.

5.

6.

"Gratitude is a virtue that you don't learn from books, and which, if lacking, may be considered a sickness of the soul." - Rabbi Adin Steinsaltz

DAY 7

Thank You Hashem for:

1.

2.

3.

4.

5.

6.

7.

But we, Your people and the flock of Your pasture, shall thank You forever; to all generations we shall recite Your praise. (Tehillim 79:13)

DAY
8

Thank You Hashem for:

1.

2.

3.

4.

5.

6.

7.

8.

Gratitude prompt: *What do you know where to get if you need it?*

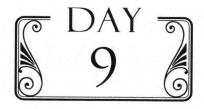

DAY
9

Thank You Hashem for:

1.

2.

3.

4.

5.

6.

7.

8.

9.

"We often take for granted the very things that most deserve our gratitude." — *Cynthia Ozick*

DAY
10

Thank You Hashem for:

1.

2.

3.

4.

5.

6.

7.

8.

9.

10.

Gratitude prompt: *What went right today?*

DAY 11

Thank You Hashem for:

1.

2.

3.

4.

5.

6.

7.

8.

9.

10.

11.

I shall praise the name of God with song, and I shall magnify
Him with a thanksgiving offering. (Tehillim 69:31)

DAY
12

Thank You Hashem for:

1.

2.

3.

4.

5.

6.

7.

8.

9.

10.

11.

12.

Gratitude prompt: What do you see right now that pleases your eye?

DAY 13

Thank You Hashem for:

1.

2.

3.

4.

5.

6.

7.

8.

9.

10.

11.

12.

13.

Gratitude prompt: *What did you read recently that touched you?*

DAY 14

Thank You Hashem for:

1.

2.

3.

4.

5.

6.

7.

8.

9.

10.

11.

12.

13.

14.

Gratitude prompt: *What did you watch recently that made you laugh?*

DAY 15

Thank You Hashem for:

1.

2.

3.

4.

5.

6.

7.

8.

9.

10.

11.

12.

13.

14.

15.

Gratitude prompt: *What homemade gift are you enjoying?*

DAY
16

Thank You Hashem for:

1.

2.

3.

4.

5.

6.

7.

8.

9.

10.

11.

12.

13.

14.

15.

16.

"Jewish prayer is an ongoing seminar in gratitude. Birkot ha-Shachar, 'the Dawn Blessings' said at the start of morning prayers each day, form a litany of thanksgiving for life itself: for the human body, the physical world, land to stand on and eyes to see with. The first words we say each morning — Modeh/Modah ani, "I thank you" — mean that we begin each day by giving thanks." - Rabbi Jonathan Sacks

DAY
17

Thank You Hashem for:

1.

2.

3.

4.

5.

6.

7.

8.

9.

10.

11.

12.

13.

14.

15.

16.

17.

Gratitude prompt: *What do you own that would
make your life harder if you didn't own?*

DAY 18

Thank You Hashem for:

1.

2.

3.

4.

5.

6.

7.

8.

9.

10.

11.

12.

13.

14.

15.

16.

17.

18.

"If a person is so obligated to be grateful to his friend for just bread, how much more so if he received a great deal of good, and ever much more so if he received from him a spiritual good, for example, he taught him wisdom or guided him on a good path and separated him from a bad one—this is a great good which nothing surpasses." — Rabbi Eliezer Papo, Pele Yoetz, Chapter 188

DAY 19

Thank You Hashem for:

1.

2.

3.

4.

5.

6.

7.

8.

9.

10.

11.

12.

13.

14.

15.

16.

17.

18.

19.

"When I started counting my blessings, my whole life turned around." — Willie Nelson

DAY 20

Thank You Hashem for:

1.   11.

2.   12.

3.   13.

4.   14.

5.   15.

6.   16.

7.   17.

8.   18.

9.   19.

10.   20.

Gratitude prompt: *What disease do you not have?*

DAY
21

Thank You Hashem for:

1.

2.

3.

4.

5.

6.

7.

8.

9.

10.

A song for a thanksgiving offering. Shout to the Lord, all the earth.
Serve the Lord with joy, come before Him with praise.
Know that the Lord is God; He made us and we are
His, people and the flock of His pasture.
Come into His gates with thanksgiving, [into] His courtyards
with praise; give thanks to Him, bless His name.
For the Lord is good; His kindness is forever, and until
generation after generation is His faith. (Tehillim 100)

DAY 21

Thank You Hashem for:

11.

12.

13.

14.

15.

16.

17.

18.

19.

20.

21.

The first word a Jew utters every day is modeh, from the same root as todah: Modeh ani l'fanekha, grateful am I for the blessing of being alive to see a new day. The order of the words, as my classmate Rabbi Shai Held has taught, is instructive. One cannot acknowledge the self — the ani, I — until one has first said modeh, thanks. - Rabbi Elliot J. Cosgrove

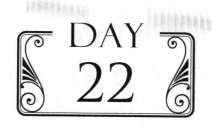

DAY
22

Thank You Hashem for:

1.

2.

3.

4.

5.

6.

7.

8.

9.

10.

11.

12.

Gratitude prompt: *What precious thing*

do you still have from your past?

DAY
22

Thank You Hashem for:

13.

14.

15.

16.

17.

18.

19.

20.

21.

22.

And she conceived again and bore a son, and she said,

"This time, I will thank the Lord! Therefore, she named him

Judah, and [then] she stopped bearing. - Bereshit 29:25

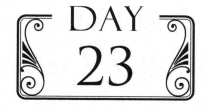

DAY 23

Thank You Hashem for:

1.

2.

3.

4.

5.

6.

7.

8.

9.

10.

11.

12.

Gratitude prompt: What did you recently

learn that you didn't know before?

DAY
23

Thank You Hashem for:

13.

14.

15.

16.

17.

18.

19.

20.

21.

22.

23.

Gratitude prompt: *What can you do that*

someone else you know can't do?

DAY 24

Thank You Hashem for:

1.

2.

3.

4.

5.

6.

7.

8.

9.

10.

11.

12.

Gratitude prompt: *What were you easily able to accomplish today?*

DAY
24

Thank You Hashem for:

13.

14.

15.

16.

17.

18.

19.

20.

21.

22.

23.

24.

"Once you get into the mode of thanking Hashem for everything, you're going to change your character. You'll become an oveid Hashem. You start loving Hashem! What is He doing for me? Everything! And once you love Hashem, the rest of the things will follow. You'll walk in His ways, you'll serve Him with all of your heart and soul; you're already sold out to Him." - Rabbi Avigdor Miller

DAY 25

Thank You Hashem for:

1.

2.

3.

4.

5.

6.

7.

8.

9.

10.

11.

12.

Gratitude prompt: *What do you have enough of?*

DAY 25

Thank You Hashem for:

13.   20.

14.
                                       21.

15.
                                       22.

16.
                                       23.

17.
                                       24.

18.

19.   25.

"Feeling grateful to Hashem is indeed our most important task. We build a steadfast connection by way of our gratitude to Him. Therefore, as long as our gratitude to Hashem is deficient, our connection to Hashem remains weak and incomplete." - Rabbi Shalom Arush, Garden of Gratitude, p. 135

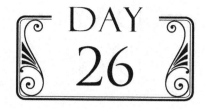

DAY 26

Thank You Hashem for:

1.

2.

3.

4.

5.

6.

7.

8.

9.

10.

11.

12.

Give thanks to the Lord because He is good, for His kindness

is eternal. (Tehillim 107:1 and 118:29 and 136:1)

DAY
26

Thank You Hashem for:

13.   20.

14.   21.

15.   22.

16.   23.

17.   24.

18.   25.

19.   26.

Gratitude prompt: *What do you have more than enough of?*

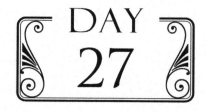

DAY 27

Thank You Hashem for:

1.   8.

2.   9.

3.   10.

4.   11.

5.   12.

6.   13.

7.   14.

"Be grateful for what you already have while you pursue your goals. If you aren't grateful for what you already have, what makes you think you would be happy with more." — Roy T. Bennett

DAY 27

Thank You Hashem for:

15.

16.

17.

18.

19.

20.

21.

22.

23.

24.

25.

26.

27.

Gratitude prompt: *What disability do you not have?*

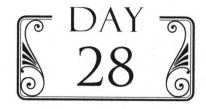

DAY 28

Thank You Hashem for:

1.

2.

3.

4.

5.

6.

7.

8.

9.

10.

11.

12.

"Though you don't have to be religious to be grateful, there is something about belief in God as creator of the universe, shaper of history and author of the laws of life that directs and facilitates our gratitude. It is hard to feel grateful to a universe that came into existence for no reason and is blind to us and our fate. It is precisely our faith in a personal God that gives force and focus to our thanks." - Rabbi Jonathan Sacks

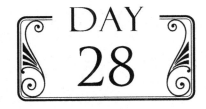

DAY 28

Thank You Hashem for:

13.   21.

14.   22.

15.   23.

16.   24.

17.   25.

18.   26.

19.   27.

20.   28.

Gratitude prompt: *Where is the blessing*
in a specific goal being thwarted?

DAY
29

Thank You Hashem for:

1.   9.

2.   10.

3.   11.

4.   12.

5.   13.

6.   14.

7.   15.

8.   16.

Gratitude prompt: *What does your income allow you to do in life?*

DAY 29

Thank You Hashem for:

17.

18.

19.

20.

21.

22.

23.

24.

25.

26.

27.

28.

29.

I will thank the Lord according to His righteousness, and I will

sing praise to the name of the Lord Most High. (Tehillim 7:18)

DAY 30

Thank You Hashem for:

1.

2.

3.

4.

5.

6.

7.

8.

9.

10.

11.

12.

13.

14.

15.

16.

Gratitude prompt: *Who sings a song that moves you?*

DAY
30

Thank You Hashem for:

17.

18.

19.

20.

21.

22.

23.

24.

25.

26.

27.

28.

29.

30.

"Gratitude will shift you to a higher frequency, and you will attract much better things." — Rhonda Byrne

DAY
31

Thank You Hashem for:

1.

2.

3.

4.

5.

6.

7.

8.

9.

10.

11.

12.

13.

14.

15.

16.

Gratitude prompt: *Who did you a favor today?*

DAY
31

Thank You Hashem for:

17.

18.

19.

20.

21.

22.

23.

24.

25.

26.

27.

28.

29.

30.

31.

Verily, the kindnesses of the Lord never cease!

Indeed, His mercies never fail! - Eicha 3:22

DAY
32

Thank You Hashem for:

1.

2.

3.

4.

5.

6.

7.

8.

9.

10.

11.

12.

13.

14.

15.

16.

Gratitude prompt: *Where in your body are you not experiencing pain?*

DAY 32

Thank You Hashem for:

17.

18.

19.

20.

21.

22.

23.

24.

25.

26.

27.

28.

29.

30.

31.

32.

"There is so much in this world for which to be grateful. Whether we choose to see that goodness, be grateful for it, and act on it, that is a choice that belongs to nobody in this world but you." - Rabbi Elliot J. Cosgrove

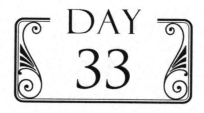

DAY 33

Thank You Hashem for:

1.

2.

3.

4.

5.

6.

7.

8.

9.

10.

11.

12.

13.

14.

15.

16.

Gratitude prompt: *What can you appreciate about getting up in the morning?*

DAY
33

Thank You Hashem for:

17.

18.

19.

20.

21.

22.

23.

24.

25.

26.

27.

28.

29.

30.

31.

32.

33.

Gratitude prompt: *Who makes you laugh?*

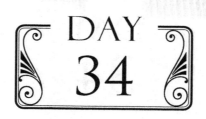

DAY 34

Thank You Hashem for:

1.

2.

3.

4.

5.

6.

7.

8.

9.

10.

11.

12.

13.

14.

15.

16.

Gratitude prompt: *How would your life be different if you couldn't swallow?*

DAY 34

Thank You Hashem for:

17.   26.

18.   27.

19.   28.

20.   29.

21.   30.

22.   31.

23.   32.

24.   33.

25.   34.

Who is rich? He who rejoices in his lot. - Pirke Avot 4:1

DAY 35

Thank You Hashem for:

1.   9.

2.   10.

3.   11.

4.   12.

5.   13.

6.   14.

7.   15.

8.   16.

Gratitude prompt: *What were you able to give someone today?*

DAY
35

Thank You Hashem for:

17.

18.

19.

20.

21.

22.

23.

24.

25.

26.

27.

28.

29.

30.

31.

32.

33.

34.

35.

Verily, the kindnesses of the Lord never cease!
Indeed, His mercies never fail! (Eicha 3:22)

DAY 36

Thank You Hashem for:

1.

2.

3.

4.

5.

6.

7.

8.

9.

10.

11.

12.

13.

14.

15.

16.

17.

18.

Gratitude prompt: *What were you able to give someone today?*

DAY 36

Thank You Hashem for:

19.

20.

21.

22.

23.

24.

25.

26.

27.

28.

29.

30.

31.

32.

33.

34.

35.

36.

What if you woke up today with only the things you thanked Hashem for yesterday? - Unknown

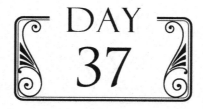

DAY 37

Thank You Hashem for:

1.

2.

3.

4.

5.

6.

7.

8.

9.

10.

11.

12.

13.

14.

15.

16.

17.

18.

Gratitude prompt: *How would your life be different if you didn't have teeth?*

DAY 37

Thank You Hashem for:

19.

20.

21.

22.

23.

24.

25.

26.

27.

28.

29.

30.

31.

32.

33.

34.

35.

36.

37.

It isn't happy people who are thankful. It's thankful people who are happy. - Unknown

DAY 38

Thank You Hashem for:

1.

2.

3.

4.

5.

6.

7.

8.

9.

10.

11.

12.

13.

14.

Gratitude prompt: *How many things can you be grateful for while shopping for groceries?*

DAY
38

Thank You Hashem for:

15.

16.

17.

18.

19.

20.

21.

22.

23.

24.

25.

26.

27.

28.

29.

30.

DAY
38

Thank You Hashem for:

31.

32.

33.

34.

35.

36.

37.

38.

*If we'll enjoy this world one hundred times a day, and if we express our gratitude to Hashem each time, that's the royal road to happiness in this world, and to the perfection in **avodas Hashem** that brings you eternal happiness in the Next World."* - Rabbi Avigdor Miller

DAY
39

Thank You Hashem for:

1.   8.

2.   9.

3.   10.

4.   11.

5.   12.

6.   13.

7.   14.

The more we thank Hashem, the happier we are.

DAY
39

Thank You Hashem for:

15.

16.

17.

18.

19.

20.

21.

22.

23.

24.

25.

26.

27.

28.

DAY 39

Thank You Hashem for:

29.

30.

31.

32.

33.

34.

35.

36.

37.

38.

39.

Gratitude prompt: *Look up and identify something*

Hashem put in the sky for you to enjoy.

DAY
40

Thank You Hashem for:

1.   8.

2.   9.

3.   10.

4.   11.

5.   12.

6.   13.

7.   14.

"Gratitude is a powerful catalyst for happiness. It's the spark

that lights a fire of joy in your soul." — Amy Collette

DAY 40

Thank You Hashem for:

15.

16.

17.

18.

19.

20.

21.

22.

23.

24.

25.

26.

27.

28.

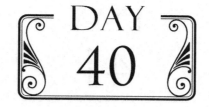

DAY
40

Thank You Hashem for:

29.

30.

31.

32.

33.

34.

35.

36.

37.

38.

39.

40.

Gratitude prompt: *What do you appreciate*

about the last garden you saw?

DAY
41

Thank You Hashem for:

1.   9.

2.   10.

3.   11.

4.   12.

5.   13.

6.   14.

7.   15.

8.   16.

DAY
41

Thank You Hashem for:

17.

18.

19.

20.

21.

22.

23.

24.

25.

26.

27.

28.

29.

30.

DAY 41

Thank You Hashem for:

31.

32.

33.

34.

35.

36.

37.

38.

39.

40.

41.

"When Leah, wife of the patriarch Jacob, had her fourth child, she named him 'Yehudah,' which means, 'I am grateful,' to reflect her gratitude to God for the gift of another son. The name Yehudah is the source of the Hebrew name of the Jewish people (Yehudim), revealing the very direct tie between Judaism and gratitude." - Dr. Alan Morinis

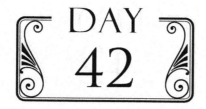

DAY
42

Thank You Hashem for:

1.

2.

3.

4.

5.

6.

7.

8.

9.

10.

11.

12.

13.

14.

DAY
42

Thank You Hashem for:

15.

16.

17.

18.

19.

20.

21.

22.

23.

24.

25.

26.

27.

28.

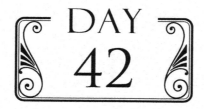

DAY 42

Thank You Hashem for:

29.

30.

31.

32.

33.

34.

35.

36.

37.

38.

39.

40.

41.

42.

Gratitude prompt: *What Jewish skill did you last use?*

DAY
43

Thank You Hashem for:

1.

2.

3.

4.

5.

6.

7.

8.

9.

10.

11.

12.

13.

14.

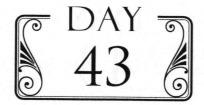

DAY
43

Thank You Hashem for:

15.   22.

16.   23.

17.   24.

18.   25.

19.   26.

20.   27.

21.   28.

DAY
43

Thank You Hashem for:

29.

30.

31.

32.

33.

34.

35.

36.

37.

38.

39.

40.

41.

42.

43.

Gratitude prompt: *What can you do for yourself that you couldn't do when you were younger?*

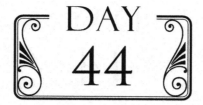

DAY 44

Thank You Hashem for:

1.

2.

3.

4.

5.

6.

7.

8.

9.

10.

11.

12.

13.

14.

DAY
44

Thank You Hashem for:

15.

16.

17.

18.

19.

20.

21.

22.

23.

24.

25.

26.

27.

28.

29.

30.

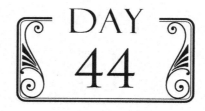

DAY
44

Thank You Hashem for:

31.

32.

33.

34.

35.

36.

37.

38.

39.

40.

41.

42.

43.

44.

"No one who achieves success does so without the help of others. The wise and confident acknowledge this help with gratitude." — Alfred North Whitehea

DAY
45

Thank You Hashem for:

1.

2.

3.

4.

5.

6.

7.

8.

9.

10.

11.

12.

13.

14.

15.

16.

DAY
45

Thank You Hashem for:

17.

18.

19.

20.

21.

22.

23.

24.

25.

26.

27.

28.

29.

30.

31.

32.

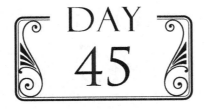

DAY 45

Thank You Hashem for:

33.

34.

35.

36.

37.

38.

39.

40.

41.

42.

43.

44.

45.

"Two kinds of gratitude: The sudden kind we feel for what we take; the larger kind we feel for what we give." — Edwin Arlington Robinson

DAY 46

Thank You Hashem for:

1.

2.

3.

4.

5.

6.

7.

8.

9.

10.

11.

12.

13.

14.

15.

16.

DAY
46

Thank You Hashem for:

17.

18.

19.

20.

21.

22.

23.

24.

25.

26.

27.

28.

29.

30.

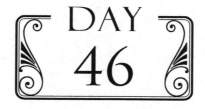

DAY
46

Thank You Hashem for:

31.

32.

33.

34.

35.

36.

37.

38.

39.

40.

41.

42.

43.

44.

45.

46.

Gratitude prompt: *What problem did you recently solve?*

DAY
47

Thank You Hashem for:

1.	9.
2.	10.
3.	11.
4.	12.
5.	13.
6.	14.
7.	15.
8.	16.

DAY
47

Thank You Hashem for:

17.

18.

19.

20.

21.

22.

23.

24.

25.

26.

27.

28.

29.

30.

31.

32.

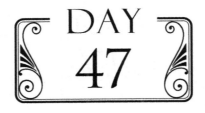

DAY
47

Thank You Hashem for:

33.

34.

35.

36.

37.

38.

39.

40.

41.

42.

43.

44.

45.

46.

47.

Gratitude prompt: *What do you have that you have taken for granted until today?*

DAY
48

Thank You Hashem for:

1.   10.

2.   11.

3.   12.

4.   13.

5.   14.

6.   15.

7.   16.

8.   17.

9.   18.

DAY
48

Thank You Hashem for:

19.

20.

21.

22.

23.

24.

25.

26.

27.

28.

29.

30.

31.

32.

33.

34.

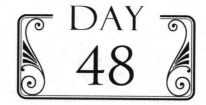

DAY
48

Thank You Hashem for:

35.

36.

37.

38.

39.

40.

41.

42.

43.

44.

45.

46.

47.

48.

DAY
49

Thank You Hashem for:

1.

2.

3.

4.

5.

6.

7.

8.

9.

10.

11.

12.

13.

14.

15.

16.

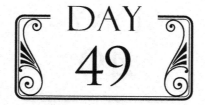

DAY
49

Thank You Hashem for:

17.

18.

19.

20.

21.

22.

23.

24.

25.

26.

27.

28.

29.

30.

31.

32.

DAY
49

Thank You Hashem for:

33.   42.

34.
                                       43.

35.
                                       44.

36.
                                       45.

37.
                                       46.

38.
                                       47.

39.
                                       48.

40.
                                       49.

41.

DAY
50

Thank You Hashem for:

1.

2.

3.

4.

5.

6.

7.

8.

9.

10.

11.

12.

13.

14.

15.

16.

DAY
50

Thank You Hashem for:

17.

18.

19.

20.

21.

22.

23.

24.

25.

26.

27.

28.

29.

30.

31.

32.

33.

34.

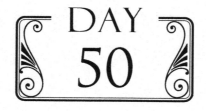

DAY
50

Thank You Hashem for:

35.   43.

36.   44.

37.   45.

38.   46.

39.   47.

40.   48.

41.   49.

42.   50.

---

*The Hebrew term for gratitude is **hakarat hatov**, which means, literally, "recognizing the good." Practicing gratitude means recognizing the good that is already yours. - Dr. Alan Morinis*

DAY
51

Thank You Hashem for:

1.

2.

3.

4.

5.

6.

7.

8.

9.

10.

11.

12.

13.

14.

15.

16.

DAY
51

Thank You Hashem for:

17.

18.

19.

20.

21.

22.

23.

24.

25.

26.

27.

28.

29.

30.

31.

32.

33.

34.

DAY
51

Thank You Hashem for:

35.

36.

37.

38.

39.

40.

41.

42.

43.

44.

45.

46.

47.

48.

49.

50.

51.

Gratitude prompt: *What were you able to give someone today?*

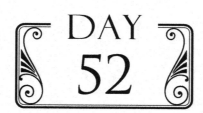

DAY
52

Thank You Hashem for:

1.

2.

3.

4.

5.

6.

7.

8.

9.

10.

11.

12.

13.

14.

15.

16.

17.

18.

DAY
52

Thank You Hashem for:

19.

20.

21.

22.

23.

24.

25.

26.

27.

28.

29.

30.

31.

32.

33.

34.

35.

36.

DAY 52

Thank You Hashem for:

37.   45.

38.   46.

39.   47.

40.   48.

41.   49.

42.   50.

43.   51.

44.   52.

___

Gratitude prompt: *What do you have because of the country you live in?*

DAY
53

Thank You Hashem for:

1.

2.

3.

4.

5.

6.

7.

8.

9.

10.

11.

12.

13.

14.

15.

16.

17.

18.

DAY
53

Thank You Hashem for:

19.

20.

21.

22.

23.

24.

25.

26.

27.

28.

29.

30.

31.

32.

33.

34.

35.

36.

DAY 53

Thank You Hashem for:

37.

38.

39.

40.

41.

42.

43.

44.

45.

46.

47.

48.

49.

50.

51.

52.

53.

Gratitude prompt: *What bad thing didn't happen to you today?*

DAY
54

Thank You Hashem for:

1.

2.

3.

4.

5.

6.

7.

8.

9.

10.

11.

12.

13.

14.

15.

16.

17.

18.

DAY
54

Thank You Hashem for:

19.   28.

20.   29.

21.   30.

22.   31.

23.   32.

24.   33.

25.   34.

26.   35.

27.   36.

DAY 54

Thank You Hashem for:

37.

38.

39.

40.

41.

42.

43.

44.

45.

46.

47.

48.

49.

50.

51.

52.

53.

54.

Gratitude prompt: *What do you own that helps you sleep at night?*

DAY
55

Thank You Hashem for:

1.   11.

2.   12.

3.   13.

4.   14.

5.   15.

6.   16.

7.   17.

8.   18.

9.   19.

10.   20.

DAY
55

Thank You Hashem for:

21.

22.

23.

24.

25.

26.

27.

28.

29.

30.

31.

32.

33.

34.

35.

36.

37.

38.

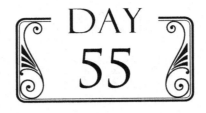

DAY
55

Thank You Hashem for:

39.

40.

41.

42.

43.

44.

45.

46.

47.

48.

49.

50.

51.

52.

53.

54.

55.

I will thank the Lord with all my heart; I will
tell all Your wonders. (Tehillim 9:2)

DAY 56

Thank You Hashem for:

1.   11.

2.   12.

3.   13.

4.   14.

5.   15.

6.   16.

7.   17.

8.   18.

9.   19.

10.   20.

DAY 56

Thank You Hashem for:

21.

22.

23.

24.

25.

26.

27.

28.

29.

30.

31.

32.

33.

34.

35.

36.

37.

38.

39.

40.

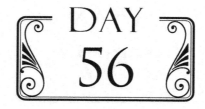

DAY
56

Thank You Hashem for:

41.   49.

42.   50.

43.   51.

44.   52.

45.   53.

46.   54.

47.   55.

48.   56.

Blessing recited upon hearing unusually good news: Blessed are You
Hashem our God, Ruler of the universe, Who is good and does good.

DAY
57

Thank You Hashem for:

1.

2.

3.

4.

5.

6.

7.

8.

9.

10.

11.

12.

13.

14.

15.

16.

17.

18.

19.

20.

DAY 57

Thank You Hashem for:

21.

22.

23.

24.

25.

26.

27.

28.

29.

30.

31.

32.

33.

34.

35.

36.

37.

38.

39.

40.

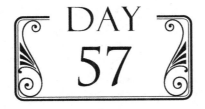

DAY
57

Thank You Hashem for:

41.

42.

43.

44.

45.

46.

47.

48.

49.

50.

51.

52.

53.

54.

55.

56.

57.

Gratitude prompt: *How many colors can you see right now?*

DAY
58

Thank You Hashem for:

1.   11.

2.   12.

3.   13.

4.   14.

5.   15.

6.   16.

7.   17.

8.   18.

9.   19.

10.   20.

DAY
58

Thank You Hashem for:

21.   31.

22.   32.

23.   33.

24.   34.

25.   35.

26.   36.

27.   37.

28.   38.

29.   39.

30.   40.

DAY
58

Thank You Hashem for:

41.

42.

43.

44.

45.

46.

47.

48.

49.

50.

51.

52.

53.

54.

55.

56.

57.

58.

Gratitude prompt: *What unpleasant or uncomfortable thing aren't you doing right now for which you can thank Hashem?*

DAY
59

Thank You Hashem for:

1.

1.

1.

2.

3.

4.

5.

6.

7.

8.

9.

10.

11.

12.

13.

14.

DAY
59

Thank You Hashem for:

15.   22.

16.   23.

17.   24.

18.   25.

19.   26.

20.   27.

21.   28.

DAY
59

Thank You Hashem for:

29.   37.

30.   38.

31.   39.

32.   40.

33.   41.

34.   42.

35.   43.

36.   44.

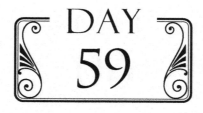

DAY
59

Thank You Hashem for:

45.

46.

47.

48.

49.

50.

51.

52.

53.

54.

55.

56.

57.

58.

59.

Gratitude prompt: *What do own that helps*
you take care of your health?

DAY
60

Thank You Hashem for:

1.

2.

3.

4.

5.

6.

7.

8.

9.

10.

11.

12.

13.

14.

15.

16.

DAY
60

Thank You Hashem for:

17.

18.

19.

20.

21.

22.

23.

24.

25.

26.

27.

28.

29.

30.

31.

32.

DAY
60

Thank You Hashem for:

33.

34.

35.

36.

37.

38.

39.

40.

41.

42.

43.

44.

45.

46.

47.

48.

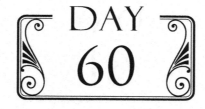

DAY
60

Thank You Hashem for:

49.   55.

50.   56.

51.   57.

52.   58.

53.   59.

54.   60.

Gratitude prompt: *What skill do you have that you use everyday?*

DAY
61

Thank You Hashem for:

1.

2.

3.

4.

5.

6.

7.

8.

9.

10.

11.

12.

13.

14.

15.

16.

DAY 61

Thank You Hashem for:

17.

18.

19.

20.

21.

22.

23.

24.

25.

26.

27.

28.

29.

30.

31.

32.

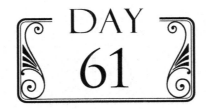

DAY
61

Thank You Hashem for:

33.

34.

35.

36.

37.

38.

39.

40.

41.

42.

43.

44.

45.

46.

47.

48.

DAY
61

Thank You Hashem for:

49.

50.

51.

52.

53.

54.

55.

56.

57.

58.

59.

60.

61.

But I, with a voice of thanks will I sacrifice to You; what I vowed I will pay, for the salvation of the Lord. (Yonah 2:10)

DAY
62

Thank You Hashem for:

1.

2.

3.

4.

5.

6.

7.

8.

9.

10.

11.

12.

13.

14.

15.

16.

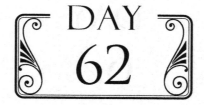

DAY
62

Thank You Hashem for:

17.

18.

19.

20.

21.

22.

23.

24.

25.

26.

27.

28.

29.

30.

31.

32.

DAY
62

Thank You Hashem for:

33.

34.

35.

36.

37.

38.

39.

40.

41.

42.

43.

44.

45.

46.

47.

48.

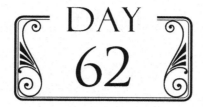

DAY
62

Thank You Hashem for:

49.	56.
50.	57.
51.	58.
52.	59.
53.	60.
54.	61.
55.	62.

Gratitude prompt: *Who did you help today?*

DAY
63

Thank You Hashem for:

1.

2.

3.

4.

5.

6.

7.

8.

9.

10.

11.

12.

13.

14.

15.

16.

DAY 63

Thank You Hashem for:

17.   25.

18.   26.

19.   27.

20.   28.

21.   29.

22.   30.

23.   31.

24.   32.

DAY 63

Thank You Hashem for:

33.

34.

35.

36.

37.

38.

39.

40.

41.

42.

43.

44.

45.

46.

47.

48.

DAY 63

Thank You Hashem for:

49.

50.

51.

52.

53.

54.

55.

56.

57.

58.

59.

60.

61.

62.

63.

Gratitude prompt: *What do you own that helps you when it's cold outside?*

DAY
64

Thank You Hashem for:

1.

2.

3.

4.

5.

6.

7.

8.

9.

10.

11.

12.

13.

14.

15.

16.

DAY
64

Thank You Hashem for:

17.   25.

18.   26.

19.   27.

20.   28.

21.   29.

22.   30.

23.   31.

24.   32.

DAY
64

Thank You Hashem for:

33.   41.

34.   42.

35.   43.

36.   44.

37.   45.

38.   46.

39.   47.

40.   48.

DAY
64

Thank You Hashem for:

49.

50.

51.

52.

53.

54.

55.

56.

57.

58.

59.

60.

61.

62.

63.

64.

Gratitude prompt: What bodily system of yours is working as it should?

DAY
65

Thank You Hashem for:

1.

2.

3.

4.

5.

6.

7.

8.

9.

10.

11.

12.

13.

14.

15.

16.

DAY
65

Thank You Hashem for:

17.

18.

19.

20.

21.

22.

23.

24.

25.

26.

27.

28.

29.

30.

31.

32.

DAY
65

Thank You Hashem for:

33.

34.

35.

36.

37.

38.

39.

40.

41.

42.

43.

44.

45.

46.

47.

48.

49.

50.

DAY
65

Thank You Hashem for:

51.

52.

53.

54.

55.

56.

57.

58.

59.

60.

61.

62.

63.

64.

65.

The Lord is my strength and my shield; my heart
trusted in Him and I was helped; my heart rejoiced and
I will thank Him with my song. (Tehillim 28:7)

DAY
66

Thank You Hashem for:

1.

2.

3.

4.

5.

6.

7.

8.

9.

10.

11.

12.

13.

14.

15.

16.

17.

18.

DAY
66

Thank You Hashem for:

19.

20.

21.

22.

23.

24.

25.

26.

27.

28.

29.

30.

31.

32.

33.

34.

DAY
66

Thank You Hashem for:

35.

36.

37.

38.

39.

40.

41.

42.

43.

44.

45.

46.

47.

48.

49.

50.

DAY
66

Thank You Hashem for:

51.

52.

53.

54.

55.

56.

57.

58.

59.

60.

61.

62.

63.

64.

65.

66.

Gratitude prompt: *What Torah thought have you had recently?*

DAY
67

Thank You Hashem for:

1.   10.

2.   11.

3.   12.

4.   13.

5.   14.

6.   15.

7.   16.

8.   17.

9.   18.

DAY
67

Thank You Hashem for:

19.

20.

21.

22.

23.

24.

25.

26.

27.

28.

29.

30.

31.

32.

33.

34.

35.

36.

DAY
67

Thank You Hashem for:

37.

38.

39.

40.

41.

42.

43.

44.

45.

46.

47.

48.

49.

50.

51.

52.

DAY
67

Thank You Hashem for:

53.

54.

55.

56.

57.

58.

59.

60.

61.

62.

63.

64.

65.

66.

67.

Gratitude prompt: *What Jewish songs do you know by heart?*

DAY
68

Thank You Hashem for:

1.

2.

3.

4.

5.

6.

7.

8.

9.

10.

11.

12.

13.

14.

15.

16.

17.

18.

DAY
68

Thank You Hashem for:

19.

20.

21.

22.

23.

24.

25.

26.

27.

28.

29.

30.

31.

32.

33.

34.

35.

36.

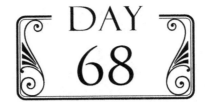

DAY
68

Thank You Hashem for:

37.

38.

39.

40.

41.

42.

43.

44.

45.

46.

47.

48.

49.

50.

51.

52.

DAY
68

Thank You Hashem for:

53.   61.

54.   62.

55.   63.

56.   64.

57.   65.

58.   66.

59.   67.

60.   68.

Gratitude prompt: *What extreme weather condition are you not experiencing?*

DAY 69

Thank You Hashem for:

1.

2.

3.

4.

5.

6.

7.

8.

9.

10.

11.

12.

13.

14.

15.

16.

17.

18.

DAY
69

Thank You Hashem for:

19.

20.

21.

22.

23.

24.

25.

26.

27.

28.

29.

30.

31.

32.

33.

34.

35.

36.

DAY
69

Thank You Hashem for:

37.

38.

39.

40.

41.

42.

43.

44.

45.

46.

47.

48.

49.

50.

51.

52.

53.

54.

DAY
69

Thank You Hashem for:

55.

56.

57.

58.

59.

60.

61.

62.

63.

64.

65.

66.

67.

68.

69.

Gratitude prompt: *What do you benefit from because of the family you were born into?*

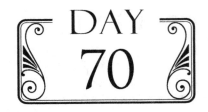

DAY
70

Thank You Hashem for:

1.

2.

3.

4.

5.

6.

7.

8.

9.

10.

11.

12.

13.

14.

15.

16.

17.

18.

DAY
70

Thank You Hashem for:

19.

20.

21.

22.

23.

24.

25.

26.

27.

28.

29.

30.

31.

32.

33.

34.

35.

36.

DAY
70

Thank You Hashem for:

37.   46.

38.   47.

39.   48.

40.   49.

41.   50.

42.   51.

43.   52.

44.   53.

45.   54.

DAY
70

Thank You Hashem for:

55.

56.

57.

58.

59.

60.

61.

62.

63.

64.

65.

66.

67.

68.

69.

70.

Someone else is happy with less than what you have. - Unknown

DAY
71

Thank You Hashem for:

1.   10.

2.   11.

3.   12.

4.   13.

5.   14.

6.   15.

7.   16.

8.   17.

9.   18.

DAY
71

Thank You Hashem for:

19.

20.

21.

22.

23.

24.

25.

26.

27.

28.

29.

30.

31.

32.

33.

34.

35.

36.

DAY
71

Thank You Hashem for:

37.

38.

39.

40.

41.

42.

43.

44.

45.

46.

47.

48.

49.

50.

51.

52.

53.

54.

DAY
71

Thank You Hashem for:

55.

56.

57.

58.

59.

60.

61.

62.

63.

64.

65.

66.

67.

68.

69.

70.

71.

Gratitude prompt: *What aspect of an upcoming holiday are you looking forward to?*

DAY
72

Thank You Hashem for:

1.   10.

2.   11.

3.   12.

4.   13.

5.   14.

6.   15.

7.   16.

8.   17.

9.   18.

Thank You Hashem for:

19.   28.

20.   29.

21.   30.

22.   31.

23.   32.

24.   33.

25.   34.

26.   35.

27.   36.

DAY 72

Thank You Hashem for:

37.

38.

39.

40.

41.

42.

43.

44.

45.

46.

47.

48.

49.

50.

51.

52.

53.

54.

55.

56.

DAY
72

Thank You Hashem for:

57.

58.

59.

60.

61.

62.

63.

64.

65.

66.

67.

68.

69.

70.

71.

72.

Gratitude prompt: *What nice place do you live close enough to that you can go visit?*

DAY 73

Thank You Hashem for:

1.

2.

3.

4.

5.

6.

7.

8.

9.

10.

11.

12.

13.

14.

15.

16.

17.

18.

19.

20.

Thank You Hashem for:

21.

22.

23.

24.

25.

26.

27.

28.

29.

30.

31.

32.

33.

34.

35.

36.

37.

38.

39.

40.

DAY 73

Thank You Hashem for:

41.

42.

43.

44.

45.

46.

47.

48.

49.

50.

51.

52.

53.

54.

55.

56.

57.

58.

DAY
73

Thank You Hashem for:

59.

60.

61.

62.

63.

64.

65.

66.

67.

68.

69.

70.

71.

72.

73.

Gratitude prompt: *How is your life better because Hashem made it possible for you to get out of bed today?*

DAY
74

Thank You Hashem for:

1.   11.

2.   12.

3.   13.

4.   14.

5.   15.

6.   16.

7.   17.

8.   18.

9.   19.

10.   20.

DAY 74

Thank You Hashem for:

21.

22.

23.

24.

25.

26.

27.

28.

29.

30.

31.

32.

33.

34.

35.

36.

37.

38.

39.

40.

DAY
74

Thank You Hashem for:

41.

42.

43.

44.

45.

46.

47.

48.

49.

50.

51.

52.

53.

54.

55.

56.

57.

58.

DAY
74

Thank You Hashem for:

59.

60.

61.

62.

63.

64.

65.

66.

67.

68.

69.

70.

71.

72.

73.

74.

Gratitude prompt: *Name a person you love who didn't suffer today.*

DAY
75

Thank You Hashem for:

1.

2.

3.

4.

5.

6.

7.

8.

9.

10.

11.

12.

13.

14.

15.

16.

17.

18.

19.

20.

DAY
75

Thank You Hashem for:

21.   31.

22.   32.

23.   33.

24.   34.

25.   35.

26.   36.

27.   37.

28.   38.

29.   39.

30.   40.

DAY
75

Thank You Hashem for:

41.   51.

42.   52.

43.   53.

44.   54.

45.   55.

46.   56.

47.   57.

48.   58.

49.   59.

50.   60.

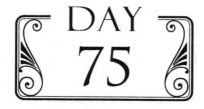

DAY
75

Thank You Hashem for:

61.

62.

63.

64.

65.

66.

67.

68.

69.

70.

71.

72.

73.

74.

75.

I will thank You in a large assembly; in a mighty

people I will praise You. (Tehillim 35:18)

DAY 76

Thank You Hashem for:

1.

2.

3.

4.

5.

6.

7.

8.

9.

10.

11.

12.

13.

14.

15.

16.

17.

18.

19.

20.

Thank You Hashem for:

21.

22.

23.

24.

25.

26.

27.

28.

29.

30.

31.

32.

33.

34.

35.

36.

37.

38.

39.

40.

DAY
76

Thank You Hashem for:

41.

42.

43.

44.

45.

46.

47.

48.

49.

50.

51.

52.

53.

54.

55.

56.

57.

58.

59.

60.

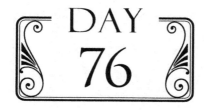

DAY
76

Thank You Hashem for:

61.

62.

63.

64.

65.

66.

67.

68.

69.

70.

71.

72.

73.

74.

75.

76.

"Give yourself a gift of five minutes of contemplation in awe of everything you see around you. Go outside and turn your attention to the many miracles around you. This five-minute-a-day regimen of appreciation and gratitude will help you to focus your life in awe." - Wayne Dyer

DAY 77

Thank You Hashem for:

1.   11.

2.   12.

3.   13.

4.   14.

5.   15.

6.   16.

7.   17.

8.   18.

9.   19.

10.   20.

DAY
77

Thank You Hashem for:

21.

22.

23.

24.

25.

26.

27.

28.

29.

30.

31.

32.

33.

34.

35.

36.

37.

38.

39.

40.

DAY

77

Thank You Hashem for:

41.

42.

43.

44.

45.

46.

47.

48.

49.

50.

51.

52.

53.

54.

55.

56.

57.

58.

59.

60.

DAY
77

Thank You Hashem for:

61.

62.

63.

64.

65.

66.

67.

68.

69.

70.

71.

72.

73.

74.

75.

76.

77.

Gratitude prompt: *What can you do with the fingers you have?*

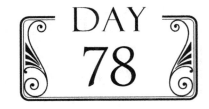

DAY
78

Thank You Hashem for:

1.   11.

2.   12.

3.   13.

4.   14.

5.   15.

6.   16.

7.   17.

8.   18.

9.   19.

10.   20.

DAY
78

Thank You Hashem for:

21.

22.

23.

24.

25.

26.

27.

28.

29.

30.

31.

32.

33.

34.

35.

36.

37.

38.

39.

40.

DAY
78

Thank You Hashem for:

41.

42.

43.

44.

45.

46.

47.

48.

49.

50.

51.

52.

53.

54.

55.

56.

57.

58.

59.

60.

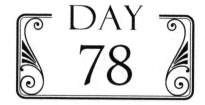

DAY
78

Thank You Hashem for:

61.

62.

63.

64.

65.

66.

67.

68.

69.

70.

71.

72.

73.

74.

75.

76.

77.

78.

Gratitude prompt: *What helpful tool do you have nearby?*

DAY 79

Thank You Hashem for:

1.

2.

3.

4.

5.

6.

7.

8.

9.

10.

11.

12.

13.

14.

15.

16.

DAY
79

Thank You Hashem for:

17.

18.

19.

20.

21.

22.

23.

24.

25.

26.

27.

28.

29.

30.

31.

32.

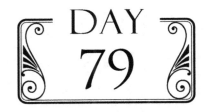

DAY
79

Thank You Hashem for:

33.

34.

35.

36.

37.

38.

39.

40.

41.

42.

43.

44.

45.

46.

47.

48.

DAY
79

Thank You Hashem for:

49.

50.

51.

52.

53.

54.

55.

56.

57.

58.

59.

60.

61.

62.

63.

64.

DAY 79

Thank You Hashem for:

65.

66.

67.

68.

69.

70.

71.

72.

73.

74.

75.

76.

77.

78.

79.

Gratitude prompt: *What has being able to read and write allowed you to accomplish in life?*

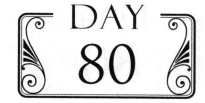

DAY
80

Thank You Hashem for:

1.

2.

3.

4.

5.

6.

7.

8.

9.

10.

11.

12.

13.

14.

15.

16.

DAY
80

Thank You Hashem for:

17.

18.

19.

20.

21.

22.

23.

24.

25.

26.

27.

28.

29.

30.

31.

32.

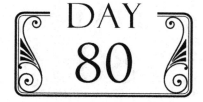

DAY
80

Thank You Hashem for:

33.

34.

35.

36.

37.

38.

39.

40.

41.

42.

43.

44.

45.

46.

47.

48.

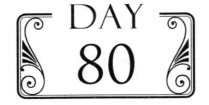

DAY
80

Thank You Hashem for:

49.

50.

51.

52.

53.

54.

55.

56.

57.

58.

59.

60.

61.

62.

63.

64.

DAY
80

Thank You Hashem for:

65.

66.

67.

68.

69.

70.

71.

72.

73.

74.

75.

76.

77.

78.

79.

80.

The more we thank Hashem, the more we will begin to

appreciate the everyday miracles. - Unknown

DAY
81

Thank You Hashem for:

1.

2.

3.

4.

5.

6.

7.

8.

9.

10.

11.

12.

13.

14.

15.

16.

DAY
81

Thank You Hashem for:

17.

18.

19.

20.

21.

22.

23.

24.

25.

26.

27.

28.

29.

30.

31.

32.

33.

34.

DAY
81

Thank You Hashem for:

35.

36.

37.

38.

39.

40.

41.

42.

43.

44.

45.

46.

47.

48.

49.

50.

DAY
81

Thank You Hashem for:

51.

52.

53.

54.

55.

56.

57.

58.

59.

60.

61.

62.

63.

64.

65.

66.

DAY
81

Thank You Hashem for:

67.

68.

69.

70.

71.

72.

73.

74.

75.

76.

77.

78.

79.

80.

81.

Gratitude prompt: *What computer skill have you mastered and how does that skill make your life better?*

DAY
82

Thank You Hashem for:

1.

2.

3.

4.

5.

6.

7.

8.

9.

10.

11.

12.

13.

14.

15.

16.

17.

18.

DAY
82

Thank You Hashem for:

19.

20.

21.

22.

23.

24.

25.

26.

27.

28.

29.

30.

31.

32.

33.

34.

DAY
82

Thank You Hashem for:

35.

36.

37.

38.

39.

40.

41.

42.

43.

44.

45.

46.

47.

48.

49.

50.

DAY
82

Thank You Hashem for:

51.

52.

53.

54.

55.

56.

57.

58.

59.

60.

61.

62.

63.

64.

65.

66.

DAY
82

Thank You Hashem for:

67.

68.

69.

70.

71.

72.

73.

74.

75.

76.

77.

78.

79.

80.

81.

82.

Gratitude prompt: *For what did Hashem give you a natural proficiency?*

DAY
83

Thank You Hashem for:

1.

2.

3.

4.

5.

6.

7.

8.

9.

10.

11.

12.

13.

14.

15.

16.

17.

18.

DAY
83

Thank You Hashem for:

19.

20.

21.

22.

23.

24.

25.

26.

27.

28.

29.

30.

31.

32.

33.

34.

35.

36.

DAY
83

Thank You Hashem for:

37.

38.

39.

40.

41.

42.

43.

44.

45.

46.

47.

48.

49.

50.

51.

52.

DAY
83

Thank You Hashem for:

53.

54.

55.

56.

57.

58.

59.

60.

61.

62.

63.

64.

65.

66.

67.

68.

DAY 83

Thank You Hashem for:

69.

70.

71.

72.

73.

74.

75.

76.

77.

78.

79.

80.

81.

82.

83.

For me, every hour is grace. And I feel gratitude in my heart each time I can meet someone and look at his or her smile. — Elie Wiesel

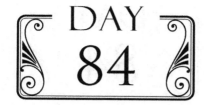

DAY
84

Thank You Hashem for:

1.

2.

3.

4.

5.

6.

7.

8.

9.

10.

11.

12.

13.

14.

15.

16.

17.

18.

DAY
84

Thank You Hashem for:

19.

20.

21.

22.

23.

24.

25.

26.

27.

28.

29.

30.

31.

32.

33.

34.

35.

36.

Thank You Hashem for:

37.

38.

39.

40.

41.

42.

43.

44.

45.

46.

47.

48.

49.

50.

51.

52.

DAY
84

Thank You Hashem for:

53.

54.

55.

56.

57.

58.

59.

60.

61.

62.

63.

64.

65.

66.

67.

68.

69.

70.

DAY 84

Thank You Hashem for:

71.

72.

73.

74.

75.

76.

77.

78.

79.

80.

81.

82.

83.

84.

Gratitude prompt: *How would your life be different if you couldn't take a deep breath whenever you want to?*

DAY
85

Thank You Hashem for:

1.   10.

2.   11.

3.   12.

4.   13.

5.   14.

6.   15.

7.   16.

8.   17.

9.   18.

DAY
85

Thank You Hashem for:

19.

20.

21.

22.

23.

24.

25.

26.

27.

28.

29.

30.

31.

32.

33.

34.

35.

36.

DAY
85

Thank You Hashem for:

37.

38.

39.

40.

41.

42.

43.

44.

45.

46.

47.

48.

49.

50.

51.

52.

53.

54.

DAY
85

Thank You Hashem for:

55.   63.

56.   64.

57.   65.

58.   66.

59.   67.

60.   68.

61.   69.

62.   70.

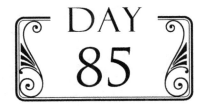

DAY
85

Thank You Hashem for:

71.

72.

73.

74.

75.

76.

77.

78.

79.

80.

81.

82.

83.

84.

85.

With generosity, I will slaughter sacrifices to You; I will thank

Your name, O Lord, because it is good. (Tehillim 54:8)

DAY
86

Thank You Hashem for:

1.

2.

3.

4.

5.

6.

7.

8.

9.

10.

11.

12.

13.

14.

15.

16.

17.

18.

DAY

86

Thank You Hashem for:

19.

20.

21.

22.

23.

24.

25.

26.

27.

28.

29.

30.

31.

32.

33.

34.

35.

36.

DAY
86

Thank You Hashem for:

37.

38.

39.

40.

41.

42.

43.

44.

45.

46.

47.

48.

49.

50.

51.

52.

53.

54.

DAY
86

Thank You Hashem for:

55.

56.

57.

58.

59.

60.

61.

62.

63.

64.

65.

66.

67.

68.

69.

70.

71.

72.

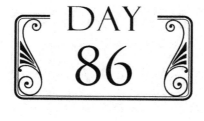

DAY
86

Thank You Hashem for:

73.

74.

75.

76.

77.

78.

79.

80.

81.

82.

83.

84.

85.

86.

Gratitude prompt: *From how many places can*

you go to get clean water to drink today?

DAY
87

Thank You Hashem for:

1.   10.

2.   11.

3.   12.

4.   13.

5.   14.

6.   15.

7.   16.

8.   17.

9.   18.

DAY
87

Thank You Hashem for:

19.

20.

21.

22.

23.

24.

25.

26.

27.

28.

29.

30.

31.

32.

33.

34.

35.

36.

DAY
87

Thank You Hashem for:

37.   46.

38.   47.

39.   48.

40.   49.

41.   50.

42.   51.

43.   52.

44.   53.

45.   54.

DAY
87

Thank You Hashem for:

55.

56.

57.

58.

59.

60.

61.

62.

63.

64.

65.

66.

67.

68.

69.

70.

71.

72.

DAY
87

Thank You Hashem for:

73.

74.

75.

76.

77.

78.

79.

80.

81.

82.

83.

84.

85.

86.

87.

Gratitude prompt: *What life lesson did a favorite teacher share with you?*

DAY
88

Thank You Hashem for:

1.

2.

3.

4.

5.

6.

7.

8.

9.

10.

11.

12.

13.

14.

15.

16.

17.

18.

DAY
88

Thank You Hashem for:

19.

20.

21.

22.

23.

24.

25.

26.

27.

28.

29.

30.

31.

32.

33.

34.

35.

36.

DAY
88

Thank You Hashem for:

37.

38.

39.

40.

41.

42.

43.

44.

45.

46.

47.

48.

49.

50.

51.

52.

53.

54.

DAY
88

Thank You Hashem for:

55.

56.

57.

58.

59.

60.

61.

62.

63.

64.

65.

66.

67.

68.

69.

70.

71.

72.

DAY
88

Thank You Hashem for:

73.

74.

75.

76.

77.

78.

79.

80.

81.

82.

83.

84.

85.

86.

87.

88.

"Gratitude is the healthiest of all human emotions. The more you express gratitude for what you have, the more likely you will have even more to express gratitude for." — *Zig Ziglar*

DAY
89

Thank You Hashem for:

1.   11.

2.   12.

3.   13.

4.   14.

5.   15.

6.   16.

7.   17.

8.   18.

9.   19.

10.   20.

DAY
89

Thank You Hashem for:

21.

22.

23.

24.

25.

26.

27.

28.

29.

30.

31.

32.

33.

34.

35.

36.

37.

38.

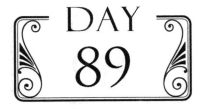

DAY
89

Thank You Hashem for:

39.

40.

41.

42.

43.

44.

45.

46.

47.

48.

49.

50.

51.

52.

53.

54.

55.

56.

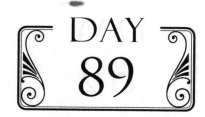

DAY
89

Thank You Hashem for:

57.

58.

59.

60.

61.

62.

63.

64.

65.

66.

67.

68.

69.

70.

71.

72.

73.

74.

DAY
89

Thank You Hashem for:

75.

76.

77.

78.

79.

80.

81.

82.

83.

84.

85.

86.

87.

88.

89.

Gratitude prompt: *How would your life be different if there were no children in it?*

DAY
90

Thank You Hashem for:

1.

2.

3.

4.

5.

6.

7.

8.

9.

10.

11.

12.

13.

14.

15.

16.

17.

18.

19.

20.

DAY 90

Thank You Hashem for:

21.

22.

23.

24.

25.

26.

27.

28.

29.

30.

31.

32.

33.

34.

35.

36.

37.

38.

DAY
90

Thank You Hashem for:

39.

40.

41.

42.

43.

44.

45.

46.

47.

48.

49.

50.

51.

52.

53.

54.

55.

56.

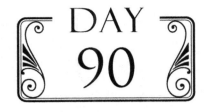

DAY
90

Thank You Hashem for:

57.

58.

59.

60.

61.

62.

63.

64.

65.

66.

67.

68.

69.

70.

71.

72.

73.

74.

DAY 90

Thank You Hashem for:

75.   83.

76.   84.

77.   85.

78.   86.

79.   87.

80.   88.

81.   89.

82.   90.

"Whereas whining delays salvation, thanking Hashem for the very problem unlock's salvation's gates. - Rabbi Shalom Arush, Garden of Gratitude, p. 136

DAY
91

Thank You Hashem for:

1.   11.

2.   12.

3.   13.

4.   14.

5.   15.

6.   16.

7.   17.

8.   18.

9.   19.

10.   20.

DAY
91

Thank You Hashem for:

21.   31.

22.   32.

23.   33.

24.   34.

25.   35.

26.   36.

27.   37.

28.   38.

29.   39.

30.   40.

DAY
91

Thank You Hashem for:

41.

42.

43.

44.

45.

46.

47.

48.

49.

50.

51.

52.

53.

54.

55.

56.

57.

58.

DAY
91

Thank You Hashem for:

59.

60.

61.

62.

63.

64.

65.

66.

67.

68.

69.

70.

71.

72.

73.

74.

75.

76.

DAY 91

Thank You Hashem for:

77.

78.

79.

80.

81.

82.

83.

84.

85.

86.

87.

88.

89.

90.

91.

Gratitude prompt: *Were you able to sleep in your own bed last night?*

DAY
92

Thank You Hashem for:

1.

2.

3.

4.

5.

6.

7.

8.

9.

10.

11.

12.

13.

14.

15.

16.

17.

18.

19.

20.

DAY
92

Thank You Hashem for:

21.   31.

22.   32.

23.   33.

24.   34.

25.   35.

26.   36.

27.   37.

28.   38.

29.   39.

30.   40.

DAY
92

Thank You Hashem for:

41.

42.

43.

44.

45.

46.

47.

48.

49.

50.

51.

52.

53.

54.

55.

56.

57.

58.

DAY
92

Thank You Hashem for:

59.

60.

61.

62.

63.

64.

65.

66.

67.

68.

69.

70.

71.

72.

73.

74.

75.

76.

DAY
92

Thank You Hashem for:

77.

78.

79.

80.

81.

82.

83.

84.

85.

86.

87.

88.

89.

90.

91.

92.

Gratitude prompt: *Name something that seemed bad at the time it happened but turned out to be good.*

DAY
93

Thank You Hashem for:

1.   11.

2.   12.

3.   13.

4.   14.

5.   15.

6.   16.

7.   17.

8.   18.

9.   19.

10.   20.

DAY
93

Thank You Hashem for:

21.

22.

23.

24.

25.

26.

27.

28.

29.

30.

31.

32.

33.

34.

35.

36.

37.

38.

39.

40.

DAY
93

Thank You Hashem for:

41.

42.

43.

44.

45.

46.

47.

48.

49.

50.

51.

52.

53.

54.

55.

56.

57.

58.

59.

60.

DAY
93

Thank You Hashem for:

61.

62.

63.

64.

65.

66.

67.

68.

69.

70.

71.

72.

73.

74.

75.

76.

77.

78.

DAY 93

Thank You Hashem for:

79.

80.

81.

82.

83.

84.

85.

86.

87.

88.

89.

90.

91.

92.

93.

"At times our own light goes out and is rekindled by a spark from another person. Each of us has cause to think with deep gratitude of those who have lighted the flame within us." — Albert Schweitzer

DAY 94

Thank You Hashem for:

1.   11.

2.   12.

3.   13.

4.   14.

5.   15.

6.   16.

7.   17.

8.   18.

9.   19.

10.   20.

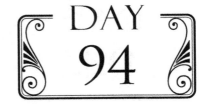

DAY
94

Thank You Hashem for:

21.

22.

23.

24.

25.

26.

27.

28.

29.

30.

31.

32.

33.

34.

35.

36.

37.

38.

39.

40.

DAY
94

Thank You Hashem for:

41.   51.

42.   52.

43.   53.

44.   54.

45.   55.

46.   56.

47.   57.

48.   58.

49.   59.

50.   60.

DAY
94

Thank You Hashem for:

61.

62.

63.

64.

65.

66.

67.

68.

69.

70.

71.

72.

73.

74.

75.

76.

77.

78.

DAY 94

Thank You Hashem for:

79.

80.

81.

82.

83.

84.

85.

86.

87.

88.

89.

90.

91.

92.

93.

94.

Blessing recited upon seeing unusual looking people or animals: Blessed are You Hashem our God, Ruler of the universe, Who makes a variety of creatures.

DAY
95

Thank You Hashem for:

1.

2.

3.

4.

5.

6.

7.

8.

9.

10.

11.

12.

13.

14.

15.

16.

17.

18.

19.

20.

DAY
95

Thank You Hashem for:

21.

22.

23.

24.

25.

26.

27.

28.

29.

30.

31.

32.

33.

34.

35.

36.

37.

38.

39.

40.

DAY
95

Thank You Hashem for:

41.

42.

43.

44.

45.

46.

47.

48.

49.

50.

51.

52.

53.

54.

55.

56.

57.

58.

59.

60.

DAY
95

Thank You Hashem for:

61.

62.

63.

64.

65.

66.

67.

68.

69.

70.

71.

72.

73.

74.

75.

76.

77.

78.

79.

80.

DAY 95

Thank You Hashem for:

81.

82.

83.

84.

85.

86.

87.

88.

89.

90.

91.

92.

93.

94.

95.

You are my God and I shall thank You; the God of my
father, and I shall exalt You. (Tehillim 118:28)

DAY 96

Thank You Hashem for:

1.   11.

2.   12.

3.   13.

4.   14.

5.   15.

6.   16.

7.   17.

8.   18.

9.   19.

10.   20.

DAY
96

Thank You Hashem for:

21.   31.

22.   32.

23.   33.

24.   34.

25.   35.

26.   36.

27.   37.

28.   38.

29.   39.

30.   40.

DAY
96

Thank You Hashem for:

41.

42.

43.

44.

45.

46.

47.

48.

49.

50.

51.

52.

53.

54.

55.

56.

57.

58.

59.

60.

DAY
96

Thank You Hashem for:

61.

62.

63.

64.

65.

66.

67.

68.

69.

70.

71.

72.

73.

74.

75.

76.

77.

78.

79.

80.

DAY 96

Thank You Hashem for:

81.

82.

83.

84.

85.

86.

87.

88.

89.

90.

91.

92.

93.

94.

95.

96.

Gratitude prompt: *Name all the types of people who were involved making it possible for you to drink your first cup of coffee today.*

DAY 97

Thank You Hashem for:

1.   11.

2.   12.

3.   13.

4.   14.

5.   15.

6.   16.

7.   17.

8.   18.

9.   19.

10.   20.

DAY 97

Thank You Hashem for:

21.

22.

23.

24.

25.

26.

27.

28.

29.

30.

31.

32.

33.

34.

35.

36.

37.

38.

39.

40.

DAY 97

Thank You Hashem for:

41.

42.

43.

44.

45.

46.

47.

48.

49.

50.

51.

52.

53.

54.

55.

56.

57.

58.

59.

60.

DAY
97

Thank You Hashem for:

61.

62.

63.

64.

65.

66.

67.

68.

69.

70.

71.

72.

73.

74.

75.

76.

77.

78.

79.

80.

DAY 97

Thank You Hashem for:

81.

82.

83.

84.

85.

86.

87.

88.

89.

90.

91.

92.

93.

94.

95.

96.

97.

Gratitude bestows reverence, allowing us to encounter everyday epiphanies, those transcendent moments of awe that change forever how we experience life and the world. — John Milton

DAY
98

Thank You Hashem for:

1.   11.

2.   12.

3.   13.

4.   14.

5.   15.

6.   16.

7.   17.

8.   18.

9.   19.

10.   20.

DAY
98

Thank You Hashem for:

21.   31.

22.   32.

23.   33.

24.   34.

25.   35.

26.   36.

27.   37.

28.   38.

29.   39.

30.   40.

DAY
98

Thank You Hashem for:

41.

42.

43.

44.

45.

46.

47.

48.

49.

50.

51.

52.

53.

54.

55.

56.

57.

58.

59.

60.

DAY
98

Thank You Hashem for:

61.

62.

63.

64.

65.

66.

67.

68.

69.

70.

71.

72.

73.

74.

75.

76.

77.

78.

79.

80.

DAY 98

Thank You Hashem for:

81.   90.

82.   91.

83.   92.

84.   93.

85.   94.

86.   95.

87.   96.

88.   97.

89.   98.

Blessing recited upon hearing thunder: Blessed are You Hashem our God,
Ruler of the universe, for His strength and His power fill the universe.

DAY
99

Thank You Hashem for:

1.

2.

3.

4.

5.

6.

7.

8.

9.

10.

11.

12.

13.

14.

15.

16.

17.

18.

DAY
99

Thank You Hashem for:

19.

20.

21.

22.

23.

24.

25.

26.

27.

28.

29.

30.

31.

32.

33.

34.

35.

36.

DAY
99

Thank You Hashem for:

37.

38.

39.

40.

41.

42.

43.

44.

45.

46.

47.

48.

49.

50.

51.

52.

53.

54.

DAY
99

Thank You Hashem for:

55.

56.

57.

58.

59.

60.

61.

62.

63.

64.

65.

66.

67.

68.

69.

70.

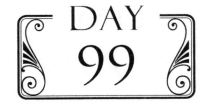

DAY
99

Thank You Hashem for:

71.

72.

73.

74.

75.

76.

77.

78.

79.

80.

81.

82.

83.

84.

85.

86.

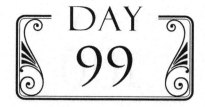

DAY 99

Thank You Hashem for:

87.

88.

89.

90.

91.

92.

93.

94.

95.

96.

97.

98.

99.

Gratitude prompt: *What valuable knowledge do you have access to because of the internet?*

DAY 100

Thank You Hashem for:

1.

2.

3.

4.

5.

6.

7.

8.

9.

10.

11.

12.

13.

14.

15.

16.

17.

18.

DAY
100

Thank You Hashem for:

19.

20.

21.

22.

23.

24.

25.

26.

27.

28.

29.

30.

31.

32.

33.

34.

35.

36.

DAY
100

Thank You Hashem for:

37.

38.

39.

40.

41.

42.

43.

44.

45.

46.

47.

48.

49.

50.

51.

52.

53.

54.

DAY
100

Thank You Hashem for:

55.

56.

57.

58.

59.

60.

61.

62.

63.

64.

65.

66.

67.

68.

69.

70.

DAY
100

Thank You Hashem for:

71.

72.

73.

74.

75.

76.

77.

78.

79.

80.

81.

82.

83.

84.

85.

86.

DAY
100

Thank You Hashem for:

87.   94.

88.   95.

89.   96.

90.   97.

91.   98.

92.   99.

93.   100.

"You must be happy and grateful to Hashem one hundred times a day!" - Rabbi Avigdor Miller

Made in the USA
Middletown, DE
13 July 2020